FRENCH-ENGLISH
Picture Dictionary

Catherine Bruzzone and Louise Millar

Illustrations by Louise Comfort and Steph Dix
French adviser: Marie-Thérèse Bougard

BARRON'S

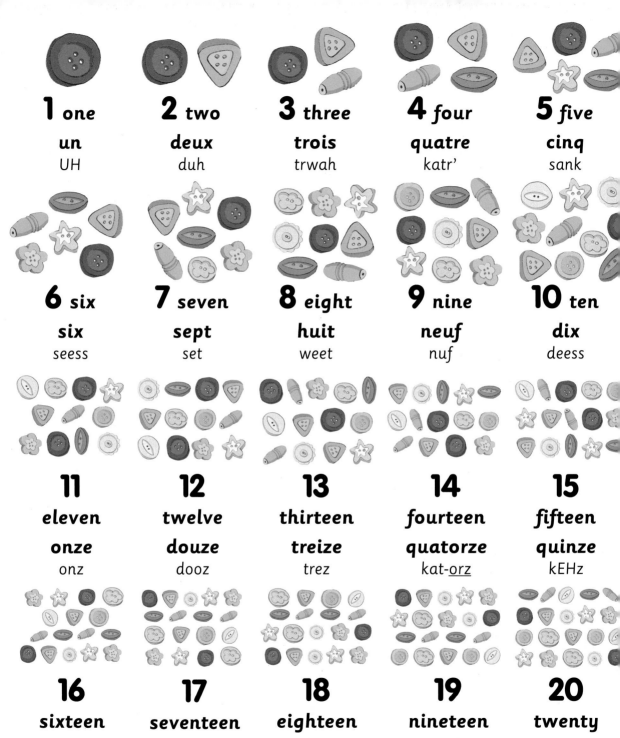

1 one
un
UH

2 two
deux
duh

3 three
trois
trwah

4 four
quatre
katr'

5 five
cinq
sank

6 six
six
seess

7 seven
sept
set

8 eight
huit
weet

9 nine
neuf
nuf

10 ten
dix
deess

11
eleven
onze
onz

12
twelve
douze
dooz

13
thirteen
treize
trez

14
fourteen
quatorze
kat-orz

15
fifteen
quinze
kEHz

16
sixteen
seize
sez

17
seventeen
dix-sept
dees-set

18
eighteen
dix-huit
deez-weet

19
nineteen
dix-neuf
dees-nuf

20
twenty
vingt
vEH

2

Contents – Table des matières

tabl' deh _mah_-tee-air

The body – Le corps

le kor

head

la tête

lah tet

eyes

les yeux

lay zyuh

nose

le nez

le nay

mouth

la bouche

lah boosh

shoulders

les épaules

lezeh-<u>pol</u>

arm

le bras

le brah

hand

la main

lah mEH

leg

la jambe

lah zhAHb

foot

le pied

le pyay

4

Clothes – Les vêtements
lay vet-m<u>AH</u>

skirt

la jupe

lah zhoop

dress

la robe

lah rub

pants

le pantalon

le pAH-tal-<u>OH</u>

coat

le manteau

le mAH-to

shirt

la chemise

lah sh-<u>meez</u>

pajamas

le pyjama

le peezhah-<u>mah</u>

shoes

les chaussures

lay showss-<u>yoor</u>

socks

les chaussettes

lay show-<u>set</u>

hat

le chapeau

le shap<u>o</u>

5

The family – La famille

lah fam_eey_

mother/Mom

la mère/maman

lah mair/ma_mAH_

father/Dad

le père/papa

le pair/pa_pah_

sister

la soeur

lah sir

brother

le frère

le frair

grandmother

la grand-mère

lah grAH-_mair_

grandfather

le grand-père

le grAH-_pair_

aunt

la tante

lah tAHt

uncle

l'oncle

lOHkl'

cousins

les cousins

lay kooz_EH_

6

The house – La maison

kitchen
la cuisine
la kwee-<u>zeen</u>

living room
le salon
le sah-l<u>OH</u>

bedroom
la chambre
lah shAHbr'

bathroom
la salle de bain
lah sal-de-<u>bEH</u>

toilet
les toilettes
lay twah-<u>let</u>

stairs
l'escalier
less-kal-yay

floor
le plancher
le plAH-<u>shay</u>

ceiling
le plafond
le plaf-<u>OH</u>

garden
le jardin
le zhar-<u>dEH</u>

7

In the house – Dans la maison

dAH lah mez-<u>OH</u>

sofa

le canapé

le kanap-<u>ay</u>

armchair

le fauteuil

le foh-<u>toy</u>

cushion

le coussin

le kooss-<u>EH</u>

curtains

les rideaux

lay reed-<u>o</u>

picture

le tableau

le tabl<u>o</u>

stool

le tabouret

le taboo-<u>reh</u>

telephone

le téléphone

8   le tay-lay-<u>fun</u>

computer

l'ordinateur

lordeenat-<u>err</u>

television

la télévision

lah tay-lay-veezee<u>OH</u>

sink

l'évier

lay-v<u>yay</u>

refrigerator

le frigo

le free-<u>goh</u>

stove

la cuisinière

lah kweezeen-<u>yair</u>

knife

le couteau

le koo<u>toh</u>

spoon

la cuillère

lah kwee-<u>yair</u>

fork

la fourchette

lah foor-<u>shet</u>

plate

l'assiette

lass-yet

glass

le verre

le vair

pot

la casserole

lah kasse<u>rul</u>

9

bed

le lit

le lee

chest of drawers

la commode

lah kum-_ud_

wardrobe

l'armoire

larm-_wah_

alarm clock

le réveil

le ray-_vay_

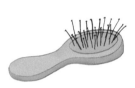

hairbrush

la brosse à cheveux

la bross ah _shvuh_

shelf

l'étagère

lay-ta-_zher_

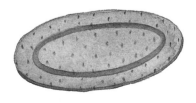

rug

le tapis

le ta_pee_

window

la fenêtre

lah f'_neht-r'_

door

la porte

lah port

The bathroom – La salle de bains
lah sal de <u>bEH</u>

**washbowl/
bathroom sink
le lavabo**
le lava<u>boh</u>

**toilet
les toilettes**
lay twah-<u>let</u>

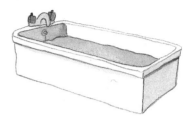

**bathtub
la baignoire**
lah beyn-<u>nwah</u>

**shower
la douche**
lah doosh

**mirror
le miroir**
le meer<u>wah</u>

**towel
la serviette**
lah sehr-vee-<u>yeht</u>

**toothpaste
le dentifrice**
le dAH-tee-<u>frees</u>

**toothbrush
la brosse à dents**
lah bruss ah <u>dAH</u>

**soap
le savon**
le sav<u>OH</u>

The city – La ville
lah veel

house

la maison

lah may-zOH

school

l'école

lay-kul

station (train/bus)

la gare

lah gaar

shop

le magasin

le mag-ah-zEN

post office

la poste

lah pust

supermarket

le supermarché

le soo-pair-marsh-ay

factory

l'usine

l'yoo-zeen

market

le marché

le mar-shay

cinema

le cinéma

le see-nay-mah

street

la rue

lah roo

sidewalk

le trottoir

le trut<u>wah</u>

bus stop

l'arrêt d'autobus

lar<u>reh</u> dow-toh-<u>boos</u>

traffic light

les feux

lay fuh

roundabout

le rond-point

le rOH-<u>pwEH</u>

streetlight

le lampadaire

le lAHpa-<u>dair</u>

road sign

le panneau

le pan-<u>o</u>

zebra crossing

le passage piétons

le pass<u>ah-zh</u> pee-eh-<u>tOH</u>

police officer

l'agent de police

lazh-AHd de pul<u>eess</u>

13

Vehicles – Les véhicules
ley veh-ee-<u>kool</u>

bus
l'autobus
low-toh-<u>boos</u>

ambulance
l'ambulance
lAHbool<u>AHss</u>

bicycle
la bicyclette
lah beesee-<u>klet</u>

car
la voiture
lah vwot-<u>yoor</u>

police car
la voiture de police
lah vwot-<u>yoor</u> de pul<u>eess</u>

motorcycle
la moto
lah moh-<u>to</u>

truck
le camion
le kam-<u>yOH</u>

fire engine
le camion de pompier
le kam-<u>yOH</u> de pOHp-<u>yay</u>

van/pickup
la camionnette
lah kam-yun-<u>net</u>

14

path

l'allée

lal-<u>ay</u>

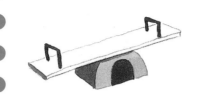

seesaw

la balançoire à bascule

lah balAH-<u>swah</u> a bas<u>kool</u>

swing

la balançoire

lah balAH-<u>swah</u>

girl

la fille

lah feey

boy

le garçon

le gar-<u>sOH</u>

child

l'enfant

lAH-<u>f</u>AH

lake

le lac

le lak

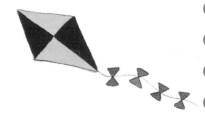

kite

le cerf-volant

le sair-vo<u>lAH</u>

bench

le banc

le bAH

15

The hospital – L'hôpital

doctor

le médecin

le mayd-<u>sEH</u>

nurse

l'infirmier

lEH-feerm-yay

x-ray

la radio

lah rad-yo

thermometer

le thermomètre

le tair-moh-<u>metr'</u>

medicine

le médicament

le may-deek-am-<u>AH</u>

bandage

le bandage

le bAH-dazh

cast

le plâtre

le platr'

crutches

les béquilles

lay bay-<u>key</u>

wheelchair

le fauteuil roulan

le fo-toy rool-AH

The supermarket – Le supermarché

egg
l'oeuf
luhf

bread
le pain
le pEH

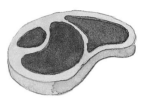

meat
la viande
lah vee-y-<u>AH</u>d

rice
le riz
le ree

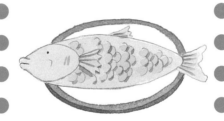

fish
le poisson
le pwah-<u>sOH</u>

butter
le beurre
le ber

milk
le lait
le lay

pasta
les pâtes
lay pat

sugar
le sucre
le s'<u>yoo</u>-kr'

Fruit – Les fruits

lay frwee

apple

la pomme

lah pum

peach

la pêche

la pesh

cherry

la cerise

lah seh-<u>reez</u>

orange

l'orange

lor-AH-zh

pineapple

l'ananas

lan-ah-<u>nass</u>

mango

la mangue

lah mAHg

banana

la banane

lah ban-<u>an</u>

grapes

les raisins

lay ray-<u>zEH</u>

strawberry

la fraise

lah frez

Vegetables – Les légumes
lay lay-g<u>oom</u>

potato

a pomme de terre

lah pum de <u>tair</u>

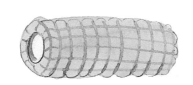

corn

le maïs

le my-<u>eess</u>

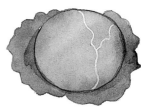

cabbage

le chou

le shoo

zucchini

la courgette

lah kor-<u>zhet</u>

carrot

la carotte

la kah-<u>rut</u>

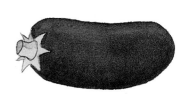

eggplant

l'aubergine

loh-bair-<u>zheen</u>

tomato

la tomate

lah to-<u>mat</u>

lettuce

la laitue

lah layt-<u>yoo</u>

celery

le céleri

le sel-air-<u>ee</u>

19

The country- La campagne

tree
l'arbre
larbr'

grass
l'herbe
lairb

flower
la fleur
lah fler

field
le champ
le shAH

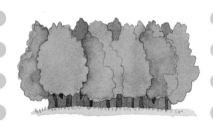

forest
la forêt
lah for<u>eh</u>

mountain
la montagne
lah mOH-ta-<u>ny</u>

bridge
le pont
le pOH

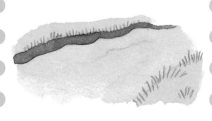

river
la rivière
lah reev-yehr

bird
l'oiseau
lwuz-<u>oh</u>

20

In the forest – Dans la forêt
dAH lah for-eh

fox
le renard
le ren-ar

squirrel
l'écureuil
lay-kooroy

deer
le cerf
le sair

rabbit
le lapin
le lah-pEH

brown bear
l'ours brun
loorss-brUH

butterfly
le papillon
le papee-oh

beetle
le scarabée
le skah-rah-bay

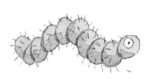

caterpillar
la chenille
lah she-nee-y

fly
la mouche
lah moosh

cat

le chat

le shah

mouse

la souris

lah soo-<u>ree</u>

dog

le chien

le shee-<u>yEH</u>

cow

la vache

lah vash

horse

le cheval

le sh-<u>val</u>

pig

le cochon

le koh-<u>shOH</u>

sheep

le mouton

le moo-<u>tOH</u>

duck

le canard

le kan-<u>ar</u>

goat

la chèvre

lah shevr

22

Baby animals – Les bébés animaux

lay bay-bay zanee-moh

puppy

le chiot

le shee-<u>oh</u>

kitten

le chaton

ler shat-<u>OH</u>

foal/colt

le poulain

le pool-<u>EH</u>

calf

le veau

le voh

chick

le poussin

le pooss-<u>EH</u>

cygnet

le bébé cygne

le bay-bay see-ny'

duckling

le caneton

le kanet-<u>OH</u>

lamb

l'agneau

lan-<u>yoh</u>

piglet

le porcelet

le porss-<u>leh</u>   23

At the beach – A la plage

ah lah plah-zh

sea
la mer
lah mair

seagull
la mouette
lah moo-_et_

sand
le sable
le sabl'

fish
le poisson
ler pwah-_sOH_

seaweed
l'algue
lalg

shell
le coquillage
le kokee_ah-zh_

rock
le rocher
le rush_ay_

sailboat
le voilier
le vwal-_yay_

wave
la vague
lah vag

Under the sea – Sous la mer

soo lah mair

octopus

la pieuvre

lah pee-yuv-<u>r'</u>

starfish

l'étoile de mer

lay-<u>twal</u> de mair

jellyfish

la méduse

lah may-<u>dooz</u>

lobster

le homard

le om<u>ar</u>

shark

le requin

le rek-<u>EH</u>

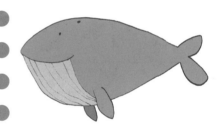

whale

la baleine

lah ba<u>len</u>

wreck

l'épave

lay-<u>pav</u>

diver

le plongeur

le plonzh-<u>err</u>

coral

le corail

le kor-<u>aye</u>

25

The zoo – Le zoo
le zoh

giraffe
la girafe
lah zheer<u>aff</u>

snake
le serpent
le sairp<u>AH</u>

hippopotamus
l'hippopotame
leepopo<u>tam</u>

dolphin
le dauphin
le doh-<u>fEH</u>

tiger
le tigre
le teegr'

crocodile
le crocodile
le kroko<u>deel</u>

polar bear
l'ours blanc
loors blAH

lion
le lion
le lee-y-<u>OH</u>

elephant
l'éléphant
laylay<u>fAH</u>

Toys – Les jouets

teddy bear

le nounours

le noo-<u>noorss</u>

robot

le robot

le roh-<u>boh</u>

ball

la balle

lah bal

puzzle

le puzzle

le puhz-<u>l'</u>

toy train

le petit train

le p'tee trEH

game

le jeu

le zhuh

doll

la poupée

lah poo-<u>pay</u>

paints

les peintures

lay pEHt-<u>yoor</u>

drum

le tambour

le tAH-<u>boor</u>   27

Party time! – C'est la fête!

seh lah fet

sandwich

le sandwich

le sAHd<u>weesh</u>

chocolate

le chocolat

le shoko<u>lah</u>

french fries

les frites

lay freet

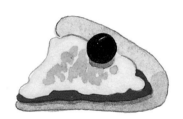

pizza

la pizza

lah peed-<u>sah</u>

cake

le gâteau

le gat<u>oh</u>

ice cream

la glace

lah glas

cola

le coca

le ko<u>kah</u>

orange juice

le jus d'orange

le zhoo d'or<u>AHzh</u>

water

l'eau

loh

28

The classroom – La salle de classe

lah sal de klass

teacher

la maîtresse

lah met-<u>ress</u>

table

la table

lah tabl'

chair

la chaise

lah shez

book

le livre

le leevr'

color pencil

le crayon de couleur

le cray-<u>OH</u> de cool-<u>err</u>

glue

la colle

lah kull

paper

le papier

le papp-<u>yay</u>

pen

le stylo

le stee<u>lo</u>

scissors

les ciseaux

lay see-<u>zoh</u>

Sports - Le sport
le spor

soccer
le football
le footbol

table tennis
le ping-pong
le peeng-pong

skiing
le ski
le skee

gymnastics
la gymnastique
lah jeem-nass-teek

cycling
le vélo
le vailo

athletics
l'athlétisme
lat-lay-tees-m

fishing
la pêche
lah pesh

swimming
la natation
lah natass-yOH

basketball
le basket
le basket

Weather – Le temps
le toh

sun
le soleil
le sol-<u>ay</u>

hot
chaud
show

rain
la pluie
lah plwee

cloud
le nuage
le noo-<u>azh</u>

wind
le vent
le vAH

storm
l'orage
lor-<u>azh</u>

fog
le brouillard
le broo-<u>yar</u>

cold
froid
frwah

snow
la neige
lah nehzh

31

Action words – Les mots d'action

lay moh daksee-yOH

to run

courir

koo<u>reer</u>

to walk

marcher

mar<u>shay</u>

to crawl

ramper

rAH<u>pay</u>

to carry

porter

por<u>tay</u>

to stand

être debout

etr' de<u>boo</u>

to sit

être assis

etr' a<u>ssee</u>

to push

pousser

poos<u>seh</u>

to hug

serrer dans ses bras

sai<u>reh</u> doh seh brah

to pull

tirer

tee<u>reh</u>

32

dragon

le dragon

le dragOH

mermaid

la sirène

lah seeren

knight

le chevalier

le sheh-valee-yeh

pirate

le pirate

le peerat

fairy

la fée

lah fay

witch

la sorcière

lah sorsee-air

prince

le prince

le prEH-ss

princess

la princesse

lah prEH-sess

castle

le château

le shato

33

digger
la pelleteuse
lah pelet-<u>uhz</u>

cement mixer
la bétonnière
lah bay-ton-<u>yair</u>

crane
la grue
lah groo

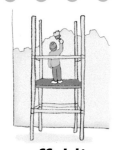

scaffolding
l'échafaudage
lay-shafo-<u>dah-zh</u>

dump truck
le camion-benne
le kam-<u>yOH</u>-ben

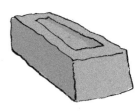

brick
la brique
la breek

bulldozer
le bulldozer
34 le bool-doh-<u>zair</u>

ladder
l'échelle
lay-<u>shel</u>

wood
le bois
le bwah

Tools – Les outils

lay-zoo-tee

rake

le râteau

le rat<u>o</u>

shovel

la pelle

lah pel

bucket

le seau

le soh

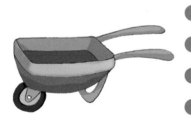

wheelbarrow

la brouette

lah broo-<u>et</u>

hammer

le marteau

le mart<u>o</u>

nail

le clou

le kloo

saw

la scie

lah see

hose

le tuyau

le twee-<u>yoh</u>

paintbrush

le pinceau

le pEH-<u>sso</u>

35

Luggage – Les bagages
lay ba<u>gah-zh</u>

suitcase
la valise
lah val<u>eez</u>

schoolbag
le cartable
le kar<u>tabl'</u>

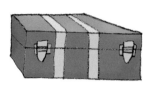

trunk
la malle
la mal

backpack
le sac à dos
le sak ah doh

handbag
le sac à main
le sak ah mEH

briefcase
la serviette
lah sair-vy<u>et</u>

basket
le panier
le pan-<u>yay</u>

shopping bag
le sac à provisions
le sak ah pru-veez-<u>yOH</u>

change purse
le porte-monnaie
le port-mon<u>eh</u>

36

Rail travel – Les voyages en train
lay vwoy-<u>ah-zh</u> AH trEH

ticket
le billet
le bee-<u>yeh</u>

conductor
le contrôleur
le kOH-tro-<u>lerr</u>

platform
le quai
le keh

engineer
la conductrice
lah kondook-<u>treess</u>

signal
le feu de signalisation
le fuh de seen-yal-eezass-<u>yOH</u>

train
le train
le trEH

seat
le siège
le see-<u>yeh-zh</u>

level crossing
le passage à niveau
le pass<u>ah-zh</u> ah neev<u>o</u>

rails
les rails
lay rah-yee

37

airplane

l'avion

lav-<u>yOH</u>

airport

l'aéroport

lah-airo-<u>por</u>

pilot

le pilote

le pee<u>lut</u>

flight attendant

l'hôtesse de l'air

loh-<u>tess</u> de lair

x-ray machine

la machine à rayon X

lah mash<u>een</u> ah rayOH eeks

passport

le passeport

le pass-<u>por</u>

hand truck

le chariot

le sharee-<u>oh</u>

snack

le casse-croûte

le kass-<u>kroot</u>

seatbelt

la ceinture de sécurité

lah sEHt-yoor de say-kyooree-<u>t</u>

At sea – En mer

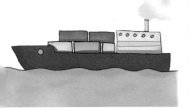

ship

le bateau

le ba<u>to</u>

yacht

le yacht

le yot

rowboat

la barque

lah bark

tanker

le pétrolier

le paytrolee-<u>yay</u>

fishing boat

le bateau de pêche

le ba<u>to</u> de pesh

ferry

le ferry

le fair<u>ee</u>

buoy

la bouée

lah boo-<u>eh</u>

port

le port

le por

lighthouse

le phare

le far

39

Opposites – Les contraires

lay kOH-<u>trair</u>

friendly

sympa

sEHpa

angry

en colère

AH kol<u>air</u>

thin

mince

mEHss

clean

propre

propr'

dirty

sale

sal

neat

bien rangé

bee-<u>ah</u> ronzh<u>eh</u>

sad

triste

treest

happy

content/contente

kOHt<u>AH</u>/kOHt<u>AH</u>t

heavy

lourd/lourde

loor/loord

Opposites – Les contraires
lay kOH-_trair_

fat
gros/grosse
groh/gross

tall
grand/grande
grAH/grAHd

short
petit/petite
p'tee/p'teet

messy
en désordre
AH day-_zordr'_

fast
rapide
rapeed

slow
lent/lente
lAH/lAHt

light
léger/légère
lay-_zheh_/lay-_zhair_

beautiful
beau/belle
boh/bel

ugly
laid/laide
leh/led

French/français – English/anglais

l'**aéroport** airport
l'**agent de police** police officer
l'**agneau** lamb
l'**algue** seaweed
l'**allée** path
l'**ambulance** ambulance
l'**ananas** pineapple
l'**arbre** tree
l'**armoire** wardrobe
l'**arrêt d'autobus** bus stop
l'**assiette** plate
l'**athlétisme** athletics
l'**aubergine** eggplant
l'**autobus** bus
l'**avion** airplane
les **bagages** luggage
la **baignoire** bathtub
la **balançoire à bascule** seesaw
la **baleine** whale
la **balle** ball
la **banane** banana
le **banc** bench
le **bandage** bandage
la **barque** rowboat
le **basket** basketball
le **bateau** ship
le **bateau de pêche** fishing boat
beau/belle beautiful
le **bébé cygne** cygnet
les **béquilles** crutches
la **bétonnière** cement mixer
le **beurre** butter
la **bicyclette** bicycle
bien rangé neat
le **billet** ticket
blanc/blanche white
bleu/bleue blue
le **bois** wood
la **bouche** mouth
la **bouée** buoy
le **bras** arm

la **brique** brick
la **brosse à cheveux** hairbrush
la **brosse à dents** toothbrush
la **brouette** wheelbarrow
le **brouillard** fog
le **bulldozer** bulldozer
le **camion** truck
le **camion de pompier** fire engine
le **camion-benne** dump truck
la **camionnette** van
la **campagne** country
le **canapé** sofa
le **canard** duck
le **caneton** duckling
la **carotte** carrot
le **cartable** schoolbag
le **casse-croûte** snack
la **casserole** pot
la **ceinture de sécurité** seatbelt
le **céleri** celery
le **cerf** deer
le **cerf-volant** kite
la **cerise** cherry
la **chaise** chair
la **chambre** bedroom
le **champ** field
le **chantier** building site
le **chapeau** hat
le **chariot** hand truck
le **chat** cat
le **château** castle
le **chaton** kitten
chaud hot
les **chaussettes** socks
les **chaussures** shoes
la **chemise** shirt
la **chenille** caterpillar
le **cheval** horse
le **chevalier** knight
la **chèvre** goat
le **chien** dog

le **chiot** puppy
le **chocolat** chocolate
le **chou** cabbage
le **cinéma** cinema
cinq five
les **ciseaux** scissors
le **clou** nail
le **coca** cola
le **cochon** pig
la **colle** glue
la **commode** chest of drawers
la **conductrice** engineer
content/contente happy
le **contrôleur** conductor
le **coquillage** shell
le **corail** coral
le **corps** body
les **couleurs** colors
la **courgette** zucchini
courir to run
les **cousins** cousins
le **coussin** cushion
le **couteau** knife
le **crayon de couleur** color pencil
le **crocodile** crocodile
la **cuillère** spoon
la **cuisine** kitchen
la **cuisinière** stove
le **dauphin** dolphin
le **dentifrice** toothpaste
deux two
dix ten
dix-huit eighteen
dix-neuf nineteen
dix-sept seventeen
la **douche** shower
douze twelve
le **dragon** dragon
l'**eau** water
l'**échafaudage** scaffolding
l'**échelle** ladder

42

école school
écureuil squirrel
éléphant elephant
en colère angry
en désordre messy
enfant child
les épaules shoulders
épave wreck
escalier stairs
étagère shelf
étoile de mer starfish
être assis to be sitting
être debout to be standing
évier sink
la famille family
le fauteuil armchair
le fauteuil roulant wheelchair
la fée fairy
la fenêtre window
la ferme farm
le ferry ferry
la fête party
le feu de signalisation signal
les feux traffic light
la fille girl
la fleur flower
le football soccer
la forêt forest
la fourchette fork
la fraise strawberry
le frère brother
le frigo refrigerator
les frites french fries
froid cold
les fruits fruit
le garçon boy
la gare station
le gâteau cake
la girafe giraffe
la glace ice cream
grand/grande tall
la grand-mère grandmother
le grand-père grandfather
gros/grosse fat
la grue crane

la gymnastique gymnastics
l'herbe grass
l'hippopotame hippopotamus
le homard lobster
l'hôpital hospital
l'hôtesse de l'air flight attendant
huit eight
l'infirmier nurse
la jambe leg
le jardin garden
jaune yellow
le jouet toy
la jupe skirt
le jus d'orange orange juice
le lac lake
laid/laide ugly
le lait milk
la laitue lettuce
le lampadaire streetlight
le lapin rabbit
le lavabo washbowl
léger/légère light
les légumes vegetables
lent/lente slow
le lion lion
le lit bed
le livre book
lourd/lourde heavy
la machine à rayon X
    x-ray machine
le magasin shop
la main hand
le maïs corn
la maison house
la maîtresse teacher
la malle trunk
maman Mom
la mangue mango
le manteau coat
le marché market
marcher to walk
marron brown
le marteau hammer
le médecin doctor
le médicament medicine

la méduse jellyfish
la mer sea
la mère mother
mince thin
le miroir mirror
la montagne mountain
la moto motorcycle
la mouche fly
la mouette seagull
le mouton sheep
la natation swimming
la neige snow
neuf nine
le nez nose
noir/noire black
le nounours teddy bear
le nuage cloud
l'œuf egg
l'oiseau bird
l'oncle uncle
onze eleven
l'orage storm
l'orange orange (fruit)
orange orange (color)
l'ordinateur computer
l'ours blanc polar bear
l'ours brun brown bear
les outils tools
le pain bread
le panier basket
le panneau road sign
le pantalon pants
papa Dad
le papier paper
le papillon butterfly
le passage à niveau level crossing
le passage piétons zebra crossing
le passeport passport
les pâtes pasta
la pêche peach
la pêche fishing
les peintures paints
la pelle shovel
la pelleteuse digger
le père father

le petit train toy train
petit/petite short
le pétrolier tanker
le phare lighthouse
le pied foot
la pieuvre octopus
le pilote pilot
le pinceau paintbrush
le ping-pong table tennis
le pirate pirate
la pizza pizza
le plafond ceiling
la plage beach
le plancher floor
le plâtre cast
le plongeur diver
la pluie rain
le poisson fish
la pomme apple
la pomme de terre potato
le pont bridge
le porcelet piglet
le port port
la porte door
le porte-monnaie change purse
porter to carry
la poste post office
le poulain foal
la poupée doll
pousser to push
le poussin chick
le prince prince
la princesse princess
propre clean
le puzzle puzzle
le pyjama pajamas
le quai platform
quatorze fourteen
quatre four
quinze fifteen
la radio x-ray
les rails rails
les raisins grapes
ramper to crawl

rapide fast
le râteau rake
le renard fox
le requin shark
le réveil alarm clock
les rideaux curtains
la rivière river
le riz rice
la robe dress
le robot robot
le rocher rock
le rond-point roundabout
rouge red
la rue street
le sable sand
le sac à dos backpack
le sac à main handbag
le sac à provisions shopping bag
sale dirty
la salle de bain bathroom
la salle de classe classroom
le salon living room
le sandwich sandwich
le savon soap
le scarabée beetle
la scie saw
le seau bucket
seize sixteen
sept seven
le serpent snake
serrer dans ses bras to hug
la serviette towel
la serviette briefcase
le siège seat
la sirène mermaid
six six
le ski skiing
la sœur sister
le soleil sun
la sorcière witch
la souris mouse
le sport sports
le stylo pen
le sucre sugar
le supermarché supermarket

sympa friendly
la table table
le tableau picture
le tabouret stool
le tambour drum
la tante aunt
le tapis rug
le téléphone telephone
la télévision television
le temps weather
la tête head
le thermomètre thermometer
le tigre tiger
tirer to pull
les toilettes toilet
la tomate tomato
le train train
treize thirteen
triste sad
trois three
le trottoir sidewalk
le tuyau hose
un one
l'usine factory
la vache cow
la vague wave
la valise suitcase
le veau calf
les véhicules vehicles
le vélo cycling
le vent wind
le verre glass
vert/verte green
les vêtements clothes
la viande meat
la ville city
vingt twenty
violet/violette purple
le voilier sailboat
la voiture car
la voiture de police police car
le voyage travel
le yacht yacht
les yeux eyes
le zoo zoo